Rainy Day
London

A Practical Guide:

100 Places to Keep Dry

Isabelle Aron

Photography by
Luke Albert

Hardie Grant

QUADRILLE

North 37

Central 11

West 59

East 105

South 83

Introduction

Striking brutalist buildings, iconic landmarks steeped in history, sharp-edged skyscrapers with shiny glass windows. London's skyline reflects the city: this is a place where old meets new, where you can immerse yourself in hundreds of years of traditions and the city's rich past, as well as exploring cutting-edge art, culture, food and drink.

The UK's capital has so much to offer – and that's true whatever the weather. While a rainy forecast will almost definitely put a dampener on a beach holiday to Majorca (speaking from experience here), there are so many things to do in London on a drizzly day that it really doesn't matter what the weather's doing. Stallholders at covered markets will continue to flog their wares, bellowing their well-rehearsed patter. Thirsty Londoners will always flock to the pub, marching along defiantly as their umbrellas turn inside out, breathing a sigh of relief when they arrive at the bar. And you can rely on the capital's museums and galleries to offer a place of refuge if the skies are grey – somewhere to spend hours exploring thought-provoking exhibitions as the rain beats down on the roof.

London is an exciting, vibrant and diverse city. Go for a wander and you'll soon see how the streets, buildings and character subtly shift as you explore, even if you're only walking for 20 minutes (with your umbrella to hand, of course). You might go from a swanky hotel bar in Mayfair to the bustling streets of Soho to make a night of it at a rowdy pub. You could start the day exploring the grand museums of South Kensington and end it by sipping incredible cocktails in an unassuming east London bar that you might easily walk past if you didn't know it was there.

While we're on the subject of drinking, London's pubs were made for rainy days – with their wood panelling, old-school bar stools and questionable carpets, the city's Victorian boozers are full of personality. They're the kind of places where you can take over a cosy corner and settle in for hours. Londoners are particularly passionate about their pubs – in fact, in some cases, punters have fought (and won) to save their locals from closure (like The Chesham Arms in Hackney – which you can read more about on page 115).

Of course, there's more to the city than pubs (although they're a great place to start). It's also home to some of the world's best museums and galleries, most of which you can access without paying a penny. And while it's hard to sum up the capital's food scene in a few sentences, let's just put it this way: you will not go hungry in this city. Whatever you fancy eating, whether it's comforting bowls of ramen, delicious pies in buttery pastry, mouth-watering desserts or something else entirely, you will find it here. You could also happily escape the elements in London's excellent shops. From iconic department stores to cute independent spots, if you want to leave laden with shopping bags (or just make one really special purchase), you're in the right place.

You may have picked up this book while taking shelter from a downpour, or perhaps you're planning ahead for a visit (it's always good to be prepared). Either way, I hope these recommendations will reassure you that London is a brilliant place to be on a rainy day.

When to travel

Everyone knows that the great British weather isn't exactly predictable – and climate change means rainfall patterns are changing long-term – but if you're planning a trip, it can be helpful to have a rough idea of what the weather *might* be doing. On average, the coldest months in London are January (8.2°C/46.9°F*), February (8.8°C/47.8°F) and December (8.6°C/47.5°F), while the warmest months are June (21°C/69.8°F), July (23.3°C/73.9°F) and August (22.9°C/73.22°F). The city is at its wettest in October (average monthly rainfall is 70.3mm), November (69.3mm), December (63.4mm) and January (62.3mm). If you're hoping to dodge the downpours, the month with the lowest average rainfall is, surprisingly, March (39.3mm). That said, when it comes to the number of rainy days per month, March sits somewhere in the middle, with around 12 days of rain** on average.

*All temperatures are the average maximum temperature

**More than 0.2mm of rain

Note: All stats are from the Met Office and are the meteorological averages for Greater London, from 1991–2020.

About this book

The 100 entries in this book are not an exhaustive list of all the things to do in London – that list would be a *lot* longer. Instead, this is a curated, rain-friendly selection – the sorts of places I would recommend to friends or family. In these pages, you'll find a mix of big cultural institutions, small independent businesses and city stalwarts that have been around for decades (and in some cases centuries).

The chapters are divided up by geographical area – central, north, west, south, east – with 20 places in each one. London is a huge city and each of these areas is fairly vast. Some places within the same chapter can be reached on foot, while others will be easy to get between on public transport or in a taxi. Within each chapter, there are four categories: Cafés & Restaurants, Pubs & Bars, Art & Culture and Shops. These have been designed with rainy days in mind, which means they are all, of course, indoors. And as rain showers have an annoying habit of turning up without warning, the book does not include any activities which would require much forward planning, such as the theatre (but if you're interested, last-minute, on-the-day tickets are usually available for most productions – some do this via TodayTix's app and website, but it varies depending on the show – check websites for details).

To make things easier when flicking through these pages, there is also a key, which includes the following categories:

☺ **Family-friendly** London has lots of brilliant things to do with children and you'll find many of them in this book. If this symbol is included, it means that there's something there that kids will enjoy – whether that's a specific bit for little ones in a museum, a children's menu at a café or a bookshop with a great selection for kids. It's also worth noting that many institutions offer free tickets for children or discounted family tickets.

✪ **Free** London is full of wonderful cultural institutions that are totally free to visit – make the most of them. Note that while some places marked 'free' won't charge an entry fee, they may host special exhibitions or events where you need to pay for tickets. Check online for specific details on prices before you visit.

⊘ **No reservations** Much-hyped new openings in London often require booking weeks or months in advance. For that reason, this book includes lots of restaurants and cafés that offer walk-ins alongside reservations, or that don't offer reservations at all. At these places, it can be worth getting there early, or you can sometimes put your name down for a table while you get a drink elsewhere, which is ideal because standing in a queue in the rain is no one's idea of fun.

⊟ **Booking ahead recommended** As mentioned, while most of the venues in this book don't require a large amount of forward planning to visit, at some of the cafés and restaurants included (plus a few of the pubs and bars), it is worth booking ahead if you can.

Most venues have online booking systems, but if the place you have your heart set on is showing no availability online, try calling up. You can also ask to be put on the waitlist. Sometimes, you'll get lucky. When it comes to cultural institutions, it varies, but some of the big blockbuster exhibitions get booked up in advance. If you just want to mooch around the permanent collection at one of the big galleries or museums, you can usually just turn up (and most of them are free). However, if it's a busy time of year (half-term, summer), you might save yourself some queuing time by booking ahead, particularly at places such as the Science Museum and the Natural History Museum. It's also worth booking ahead for cinemas – if only so you can choose a decent seat.

Getting around

Public transport

While you can, in theory, drive around London, there's a high chance you'd spend a lot of time sitting in traffic, especially if you're trying to navigate central London. Driving can also be an expensive way to travel because of parking costs, the Congestion Charge and the Ultra Low Emission Zone (ULEZ) charge. Check the Transport for London (TfL) website for more information. With that in mind, the best way to explore the capital is by using public transport. The TfL network is excellent and covers a lot of ground. Transport options include buses, the Tube, the Overground, the DLR, trams, trains and the east–west Crossrail: the Elizabeth Line. The Tube map (famously designed by Harry Beck, which you can learn all about at the London Transport Museum – read more about that on p27) shows how all of these lines intersect (not including bus routes). It's a system that's designed to be easy to navigate, even if you're a first-time visitor, but if you're struggling, do ask a TfL member of staff or a friendly Londoner (forget the stereotype, plenty of them do exist!). Head to tfl.gov.uk or download the TfL Go app for status updates, maps and to plan your journey. If you prefer to hold an actual map in your hands, look out for hard copies at TfL stations.

Other useful apps to have are Google Maps and Citymapper. The latter is particularly handy, as route options include insider knowledge, such as which part of the tube carriage to aim for so that you're in the best position for a smooth exit or changing to a different platform when you get off. TfL's journey planner, Google Maps and Citymapper all have the option to filter routes by particular types of transport, or for step-free and wheelchair-accessible journeys.

Cycling

Travelling on two wheels might not be the first choice for everyone in the rain, but if it's only showers, then cycling is a good option. TfL has its own bike hire scheme, Santander Cycles. It has good coverage around the city, with more than 12,000 bikes at around 800 docking stations. You can find your nearest docking station on the TfL website or using the Santander Cycles app. There's a flat-fee for a 30-minute ride, making it ideal for short bursts of cycling throughout the day. You can also hire bikes through Lime (the bikes are lime green, so they're easy to spot) – find out more through the Lime app. Lime bikes are also available to hire through the Uber app. Note that all the bike hire schemes are BYOH – that's bring your own helmet. All rental bikes have lights and mudguards, but you might also want a waterproof, for obvious reasons.

Taxis

There are two types of taxis in London – black cabs and minicabs. You can hail black cabs on the street, find one at a designated taxi rank or pre-book one (but be aware that this will cost slightly more). Black cabs are usually the most expensive taxi option – they are metered and there's a minimum starting fee. Minicabs need to be booked in advance and you can check TfL's website to confirm they are licensed. There's also a wealth of taxi apps, including Uber, Bolt and FreeNow.

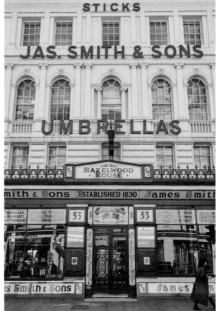

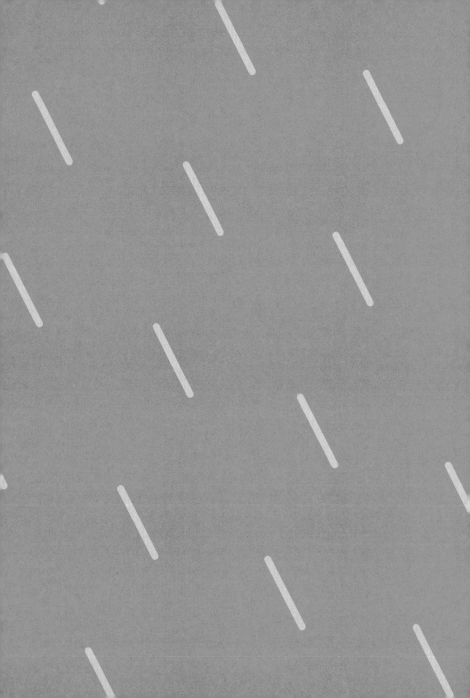

Central

Buckingham Palace, Big Ben, St Paul's Cathedral – central London might be known for its iconic landmarks but there's way more to this area than famous sights. Always buzzing, Soho is known for its vibrant restaurants and bars, as well as being a popular nightlife spot and LGBTQ+ hub. Towards Hyde Park, Mayfair is where you'll find high-end shops and swanky places to eat and drink, while the City of London is the financial district, home to skyscrapers like The Gherkin and The Cheesegrater (yes, they all have silly nicknames). Of course, this is one of the best cities in the world for culture, too – from the theatres of the West End to major institutions along the South Bank.

Seven Dials Market

If you're indecisive when it comes to food, you may need to do a few laps of this vast Covent Garden food hall before you order anything. Bigger than it looks from the outside, Seven Dials Market has more than 15 different stalls over two floors, which is ideal if you want to try a few different things or if not everyone you're with wants to eat the same thing. Order from the individual stalls and you'll get a buzzer which will flash when your food is ready. In the meantime, grab a drink from the bar and take a seat at one of the (mostly communal) tables. A few places have their own seating, including Pick & Cheese, which serves top-quality cheese from a sushi-style conveyor belt – it's basically heaven for fromage fans. The market is great for a shopping pitstop or a casual and affordable dinner, but you might find you don't want to leave in a hurry and that's fine, too.

35 Earlham Street, WC2H 9LX
sevendialsmarket.com
@sevendialsmkt
☺ ⊘

Kiln

Kiln

Forget gas or electricity – in the open kitchen at this narrow Soho eatery, almost everything is cooked in a wood-burning kiln oven or on flame-powered grills, making it an excellent place to warm up if you've been caught in a downpour. Kiln's Thai-inspired menu of spicy and fragrant dishes should also help take the chill off (be warned: the spice level isn't for the faint-hearted, but they can adapt dishes if you want to take it down a notch). The menu is filled with creative regional Thai dishes made using British ingredients, but the Clay Pot Baked Glass Noodles with Tamworth Pork Belly and Crab Meat is a must-order dish. Book ahead if you can, or arrive early for a walk-in spot (12pm for lunch and before 7pm for dinner). The counter seats, often reserved for walk-ins, offer a front-row seat to all the action in the kitchen.

58 Brewer Street, W1F 9TL
kilnsoho.com
@kilnsoho

St John

With white walls and white tablecloths, the decor at this famed Smithfield restaurant is pretty minimalist, leaving the food to speak for itself. And boy, does it. St John is known for being a pioneer of nose-to-table cooking, so expect dishes involving offal and lesser-used cuts of meat. For the less adventurous, there are also some fantastic fish dishes. The menu changes daily, but there are some classic plates that are always available – like the Roast Bone Marrow and Parsley Salad or the hefty slab of Welsh Rarebit. The food is hearty and the portions are pretty generous (price-wise, mains range from around £20 to £30). If you can manage dessert, the madeleines will require 15 minutes of patience (they're made to order), but they're definitely worth the wait.

26 St John Street, EC1M 4AY
Other locations: Marylebone, Spitalfields
stjohnrestaurant.com
@st.john.restaurant

Bao Fitz

This cult restaurant made Londoners go wild for bao buns when it launched its first branch back in 2015. Punters queued around the block to try Bao's Tawainese-inspired street food, especially its steamed buns. Thankfully, it now has five restaurants and while the original Soho spot has its charm, the Fitzrovia branch is bigger (walk-ins are available or you can book ahead). The decor here is minimalist and most of the seating is around a wooden, u-shaped bar. The drinks list features unusual cocktails (Sweet Potato Sour, anyone?) and creative alcohol-free options. As for the food, the pillowy bao buns are the stars here – don't miss the Classic (braised pork, fermented greens and peanut powder) and the Cod Black, which is unique to this branch. You'll also find small plates, mains and sides on the menu, including Taiwanese Fried Chicken and Beef Cheek Nuggets. Make sure you save room for dessert, though – its sweet, deep-fried bun with malty Horlicks ice cream is legendary.

31 Windmill Street, W1T 2JN
Other locations: Borough, King's Cross, Shoreditch, Soho
baolondon.com
@bao_london

The Wolseley

An old car showroom might sound like an unlikely location for a chic all-day eatery, but that's the story behind The Wolseley. Built in 1921 as the grand home of Wolseley Motors Limited, this beautiful space was transformed into a restaurant in 2003, keeping original features such as its domed ceiling and chequerboard marble flooring. Inspired by the European grand cafés, The Wolseley offers breakfast, lunch, dinner, afternoon tea and an all-day and late-night menu. Coming here feels like a real treat, but it's not stuffy and the menu won't blow your budget (lots of mains hover around the £20 mark and there's a fixed price menu which includes three courses for £31.50). Plus, there's no dress code, which keeps things relaxed. Book ahead if you can (especially for afternoon tea), but walk-ins are available throughout the day. Need an alternative? Its wonderful sister restaurant Brasserie Zédel is a 10-minute walk away and serves up affordable French brasserie-style food in elegant Art Deco surroundings.

160 Piccadilly, W1J 9EB
thewolseley.com
@thewolseley

The Wolseley

The French House

The French House

A word of warning – don't try and order a pint at this Soho institution. Rich in history and full of character, one of the many loveable quirks of The French House is that it only sells half-pints (they make an exception on April 1st). Originally known as the York Minster, the pub became a meeting point for the French Resistance during the Second World War – army officer Charles de Gaulle is said to have hung out here when he escaped to London. It's also been a popular place for creative minds to meet – artist Francis Bacon was a regular and poet Dylan Thomas allegedly once left his manuscript for *Under Milk Wood* beneath a chair here. Now, it's still a much-loved pub with a buzzy atmosphere. Look out for the sign that asks punters not to talk on their phones 'in the interests of good conversation and serious drinking'. If you're hungry, you might get a seat at the brilliant restaurant upstairs (or you can book ahead), where some of London's top chefs have cut their teeth.

49 Dean Street, W1D 5BG
frenchhousesoho.com
@frenchhousesoho

The Connaught Bar

Two words: Martini Trolley. That's what The Connaught Bar in Mayfair is most famous for. Part of The Connaught Hotel, this is one of London's most renowned drinking spots. The bar's Martini is its most popular drink – order one and you'll not only get an expertly-crafted cocktail, but something close to a theatrical performance, too. The trolley is wheeled over to your table, stacked with gin, the house blend of dry vermouths and a selection of bitters. Tailored to your tastes, the mixologist uses pipettes to add bitters, pours gin from a dramatic height and swishes around a lemon peel as it's added to the glass to infuse the drink. Admittedly, the drinks aren't cheap (most cocktails are £20+), so you might not want to stay here all night. But having one or two drinks in this glamorous bar, with its embellished ceilings and plush green leather seats, is a special experience. Plus, you get a complimentary welcome drink and bowls of snacks, which they're quick to refill.

The Connaught Hotel,
Carlos Place, W1K 2AL
the-connaught.co.uk
@theconnaught

Gordon's Wine Bar

Hidden in a subterranean vault with curved ceilings and tables lit by flicking candlelight, Gordon's Wine Bar is the perfect spot to escape the elements. Opened in 1890 and thought to be London's oldest wine bar, this city stalwart feels like a time capsule. The walls are covered in framed historical newspaper clippings, including one from Queen Elizabeth II's coronation. As well as a cosy ambience, come for the impressive wine selection, which ranges from full-bodied French reds to natural orange wines to sherry and port. If you can't get a table inside, there's a long stretch of outdoor space with heated awnings to keep you warm and dry. The food menu is mostly cold meats and cheeses from the bar's very well-stocked fridge. Choose from mezze platters or build your own cheese board. Not sure what to order? Let the menu's wine pairing recommendations guide you. But really, you can't go too wrong with wine and cheese.

47 Villiers Street, WC2N 6NE
gordonswinebar.com
@gordonswinebar

Lyaness

Lyaness

Whatever you order at this chic cocktail bar with views over the Thames, you're in good hands. The brains behind Lyaness is Ryan Chetiyawardana, AKA Mr Lyan, a cocktail genius who's won countless awards for his creations. The menu changes, but it celebrates unusual ingredients, using them to create twists on classics (such as a slightly savoury take on a G&T or a fancy version of a Piña Colada), as well as totally new concoctions. If you're unsure what to order, the bar's friendly staff are on hand to help you decide. Sit at the grand marble bar to watch the mixologists at work, or grab a seat by the window for people-watching along the South Bank.

**Sea Containers London,
20 Upper Ground, SE1 9PD
lyaness.com
@lyanessbar**

Swift

An award-winning bar on Soho's Old Compton Street, Swift has a bit of a split personality. But that's a good thing – you get two very different bars under one roof. The ground floor has a more casual vibe, serving up aperitifs, fun cocktails (including a good non-alcoholic selection), wine and beer. The bar's signature drink is the Swift Irish Coffee – a mix of Jameson whiskey, Swift's own coffee blend, demerara sugar, cream and nutmeg. And if you're popping in after dinner, the Sgroppino doubles as dessert – with prosecco and St Germain poured over lemon sorbet. Downstairs, there's a dimly-lit basement bar with a different menu, featuring more experimental drinks and 300 different types of whiskey. Upstairs, it's easy enough to just pop in, but you should book for the basement bar (staff recommend getting a table for at least two hours). Whichever bar you choose, you'll want to stay for more than a swift one.

**12 Old Compton Street, W1D 4TQ
Other locations: Shoreditch, Borough
barswift.com
@swiftbars**

Barbican Centre

This iconic Brutalist building is pretty much a one-stop shop for all your cultural needs. With three cinema screens, two theatres, two art galleries and a concert hall, the Barbican Centre's diverse programme covers film, art, photography, theatre, music and dance. It's also home to the London Symphony Orchestra, which performs here 70 times a year, but there's plenty of contemporary music on offer, too. There are several places to eat and drink, as well as libraries where you can peruse the books or get lost in classic vinyl at the listening station. Don't miss the foliage-filled conservatory (check the website for opening times) – you can wander around and admire the greenery or book ahead to enjoy a drink and snacks at the bar in its lush surroundings.

Silk Street, EC2Y 8DS
barbican.org.uk
@barbicancentre
☺ ✩

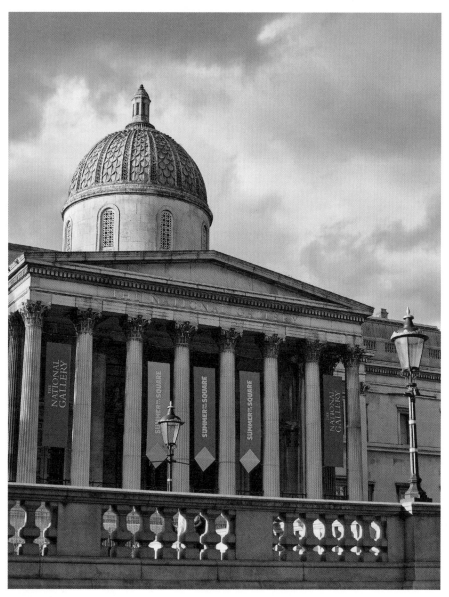

National Gallery

The National Gallery

With more than 2,300 artworks spanning 700 years from the 13th century to the early 20th century, there's a lot to see at The National Gallery. You could pop in to admire a specific painting (Van Gogh's 'Sunflowers', for example) or devote a whole day to exploring everything from Medieval classics to French impressionists. If you feel overwhelmed by the scale of it, the gallery has plotted out three handy routes which take between 25 and 35 minutes, covering different eras. The permanent collection is free to visit, but you'll need to buy a ticket to see its regularly changing big exhibitions. There are often free talks, drawing sessions and events for kids. As well as the world-class art, the building's mosaic floors and ornate ceilings are a thing of beauty too.

Trafalgar Square, WC2N 5DN
nationalgallery.org.uk
@nationalgallery
☺ ✪

London Transport Museum

Not just a way of getting around the capital, London's public transport system has a fascinating history and is known for its ground-breaking design. The London Transport Museum charts the evolution of transport in the city in a way that will entertain both adults and kids – exhibits include a horse-drawn omnibus, the world's first underground steam train from the 1860s and the first-ever tube map. The All Aboard playzone for kids aged 0–7 features loads of interactive activities, including uniforms to dress up in, a mini lost property office and a mini fleet of vehicles. For transport fans of all ages, there's the chance to get into a bus driver's cabin and have a go on a tube driving simulator. Doing your own announcements is optional, but encouraged.

Covent Garden Piazza, WC2E 7BB
ltmuseum.co.uk
@ltmuseum
☺

Southbank Centre

Whether you're a born-and-bred Londoner or it's your first trip to the capital, walking along the South Bank always feels special – even if it is a bit drizzly. As well as views over the Thames, you'll see some of London's biggest landmarks – Big Ben, St Paul's and skyscrapers like The Cheesegrater and The Walkie Talkie. It's also where you'll find the UK's biggest arts centre, the Southbank Centre. The multi-venue space includes the Royal Festival Hall, with its 2,500-seat auditorium, the National Poetry Library and a singing lift. Next door, there's the Hayward Gallery and more performance spaces in the Queen Elizabeth Hall and Purcell Room. Its programme includes blockbuster gigs and exhibitions, special seasons often curated by big names and annual events such as Women of the World festival. It's also the sort of place where you can just pop in and find something fun going on – free talks, gigs, poetry, art installations and sessions for kids are often on the agenda.

Belvedere Road, SE1 8XX
southbankcentre.co.uk
@southbankcentre
☺ ✪

Tate Modern

'Free and open to all' – that's the message that's proudly displayed on the side of this world-class art gallery. Housed in the former Bankside Power Station, Tate Modern is an imposing building that's worth your attention, even before you get to the artwork inside its walls. The seven-storey space has an incredible collection of modern and contemporary art and with so much to offer, it can be hard to know where to start. To help with that, there are free guided tours, helpful guides for families and activities for kids. The 'Start display' acts as a good jumping-off point and offers some questions to think about as you look at artworks around the gallery. You'll need to buy a ticket for its temporary exhibitions, but the permanent collection includes works from the likes of Yves Klein, Henri Matisse and Pablo Picasso – and it's all totally free.

Bankside, SE1 9TG
tate.org.uk
@tate
☺ ✪

Tate Modern

Daunt Books

Daunt Books

Just as you shouldn't judge a book by its cover, you probably shouldn't judge a bookshop by its shopfront, but it's hard to deny that Daunt Books is particularly aesthetically pleasing. A beautiful Edwardian bookshop, it has a charming wooden exterior and big windows filled with colourful titles. Said to be the first custom-built bookshop in the world, it was taken over by James Daunt in 1990 and specializes in literature and travel. Fiction, greeting cards and wrapping paper are in the front, but the most unique space is at the back. Dark wooden balconies, ornate green lamps, a stained glass window, a conservatory ceiling and, of course, tall shelves stacked with books make this a strong contender for the city's prettiest bookshop. Here, over three floors, titles are arranged by country, but it's more than just guide books – there's also fiction, history, travelogues and more. Look out for special talks and events and don't leave without a signature Daunt tote bag.

84 Marylebone High Street, W1U 4QW
Other locations: Belsize Park, Hampstead, Holland Park, Cheapside
dauntbooks.co.uk
@dauntbooks

Fortnum & Mason

Huge wheels of parmesan. Hundreds of chocolate truffles. An elaborate perfume counter. Walking around Fortnum & Mason is a total sensory overload. And while you *could* fork out thousands of pounds here, you could also just spend hours walking around the iconic department store's five floors and taking it all in without spending a penny. Whether you want to splash out on a silk scarf or you're after a tin of Fortnum & Mason's tea, the shopping possibilities here are endless. If you need a breather from retail therapy, there are various bars and cafés for cocktails, afternoon tea or a light bite. Got a sweet tooth? Treat yourself to the legendary knickerbocker glory at The Parlour.

181 Piccadilly, W1A 1ER
fortnumandmason.com
@Fortnums

James Smith & Sons Umbrella Shop

Caught in a downpour in central London and need a brolly? Swerve the tourist stalls flogging novelty Union Jack-clad ones and head to James Smith & Sons Umbrella Shop. Dating back to 1830, this family business has set up shop in a few different locations over the years, including a site on Saville Place which was so small that customers who wanted to open up an umbrella had to step outside. One of London's oldest shops, the New Oxford Street branch opened in 1857 and more than 160 years later, its Victorian shopfront is largely unchanged. Even if you don't actually need anything, it's worth a look to see the walls lined with umbrellas and walking sticks with ornate wooden handles carved to look like cute animals.

53 New Oxford Street, WC1A 1BL
james-smith.co.uk
@jamessmith1830

Liberty

Liberty

Arthur Lasenby Liberty opened his department store with three members of staff and a £2,000 loan from his future father-in-law. His vision? To 'metaphorically dock a ship' on the city's streets, bringing luxury goods and fabrics from all over the world to London. The store opened in 1875, but in 1924, he had enough cash to construct the (now Grade II-listed) Tudor-style building, made from the wood of old battleships. Set over six floors, with three grand atriums and interconnecting rooms, exploring the store feels a bit like wandering around a grand old house. Except that it's filled with beautiful things to buy – huge rugs piled high, reams of Liberty fabric on the haberdashery floor, shelves filled with crockery and homeware and lots more. You could stay here all day, but if you want yet more retail therapy, dodge the showers as you hop between Carnaby Street's shops, or take a break at nearby Kingly Court's many restaurants and bars.

Regent Street, W1B 5AH
libertylondon.com
@libertylondon

Selfridges

You know how department stores often have the perfume counter at the front? That all started at Selfridges, one of London's most famous shops. Founded by Harry Gordon Selfridge in 1908, he wanted it to be easier for customers to try perfume and beauty products (usually found in the back). Plus, it also masked the not-so-nice smells coming from horses pulling carts along busy Oxford Street. The sweet smells of the perfume counter still greet you as you walk through the doors of Selfridges today, while elsewhere there's a huge selection of fashion, homeware, food and drink, beauty, jewellery and tech across its six floors. Need to rest your legs? There are plenty of food and drink spots, ranging from a Champagne and oyster bar to Neapolitan slices at Pizza Pilgrims. There's even a cinema. Mr Selfridge would approve. After all, his original ethos was all about making shopping a pleasure rather than a chore.

400 Oxford Street, W1A 1AB
selfridges.com
@theofficialselfridges

North

Brilliant cafés and restaurants, excellent pubs, cute shops – there's no shortage of things to do in north London. But thanks to its many hills and leafy neighbourhoods, some parts of it – such as Crouch End, Hampstead and Highgate – almost feel like little villages. This part of town is also home to one of the city's longest thoroughfares, Green Lanes, a 6.3-mile stretch that's full of vibrant Turkish restaurants, cafés and bakeries – particularly between Turnpike Lane tube station and Harringay Green Lanes Overground station, known as the Harringay Ladder. More central is bustling Islington and rejuvenated King's Cross, which as well as being a major transport hub, is full of shops and great places to eat and drink.

The Dusty Knuckle

The Dusty Knuckle

There's never a bad time of day to visit this buzzy independent bakery and restaurant. Whether you want pastries for breakfast, sandwiches for lunch or pizzas and small plates for dinner, The Dusty Knuckle has you covered. It all started in its original branch in Dalston, but the Green Lanes location has more indoor space if the weather isn't on your side. The menu varies but you're guaranteed to sample quality ingredients and excellent flavour combinations. This place is also a social enterprise and runs a scheme to help rehabilitate young people at risk, so you'll be doing some good while you're eating baked goods.

429 Green Lanes, N4 1AH
Other locations: Dalston
thedustyknuckle.com
@thedustyknuckle

Westerns Laundry

Written in chalk on a blackboard, the menu at this ace neighbourhood restaurant in Drayton Park is ever-changing but always delicious. The focus at Westerns Laundry is fish, but the menu also includes some veggie and meat dishes. It all comes in the form of enticing plates of food designed for sharing (prices vary depending on the ingredients used, but larger dishes can be around £30). Save room for dessert, too – and if the brilliantly boozy Rum Baba is on the menu, order it. With full-length glass doors, the space is flooded with light by day, while at night time, candle-lit tables make for a cosy atmosphere. On the drinks front, it's all about natural and low-intervention wine, and staff are on hand to offer advice should you need it. They make a mean Negroni, too.

34 Drayton Park, N5 1PB
Other locations: Big Jo, Finsbury Park; Jolene, Stoke Newington; Primeur, Stoke Newington
westernslaundry.com
@westernslaundry

Max's Sandwich Shop

At this much-loved spot in Crouch Hill, Max Halley serves up the kind of food that you'll be thinking about long after you've finished your last bite. All served on homemade focaccia (don't mention sourdough, he's not a fan), the sandwiches here are stacked high with creative fillings that will kick your taste buds into overdrive. The Ham, Egg 'N' Chips with slow-cooked ham hock and crispy shoestring fries is a classic, but Max has also been known to fill sarnies with spring rolls, lasagne and Bombay mix (not all in the same sandwich, don't worry). Depending on the day of the week, it's open for brunch, lunch and dinner (but the menu is the same). Max will usually be there serving up his creations and endless cups of coffee – or cocktails, if you fancy something stronger.

19 Crouch Hill, N4 4AP
maxssandwichshop.com
@lunchluncheon

Xi'an Impression

In an unlikely location opposite the Emirates Stadium, you'll find Xi'an Impression, a low-key BYOB restaurant serving up some of the best Chinese food in London. Specializing in street food from Xi'an, the capital of Shaanxi Province in northern China, its signature dish is the biang biang noodles – long ribbons of wide wheat noodles, which are hand-pulled and served in a spicy sauce that's totally addictive. Other gems include the Xi'an cold noodles and the Xi'an burgers, but you can't order badly here. It's not a huge restaurant so it's worth going early and avoiding Arsenal match days to nab a table. And no matter how careful you are, you'll almost definitely flick sauce on yourself, so grab a stack of napkins – and maybe don't wear white.

117 Benwell Road, N7 7BW
xianimpression.co.uk
@Xianimpression

Sambal Shiok

The laksa at Sambal Shiok might just be one of the most comforting bowls of food in the city. And thanks to the restaurant's open kitchen, you'll smell the fiery and fragrant broth as soon as you walk through the door. You can choose your toppings (chicken, prawn, tofu, vegetables) and there's also a vegan broth made without shrimp. All options come with deep-fried tofu puffs, which are basically flavour sponges for all that mouth-watering liquid – they will win over even tofu sceptics. The default spice option is 'hot', but you can opt for 'medium' if you prefer less of a kick (or ask for extra coconut milk). The portions are generous, so come hungry – and know that ordering the Malaysian Fried Chicken with Peanut Sauce to start is never a bad idea.

171 Holloway Road, N7 8LX
sambalshiok.co.uk
@sambalshiok

The Pineapple

Painted bright turquoise and with ornate pineapples above its windows, it's hard to miss this popular Kentish Town pub, even if it is hidden away on a residential street. A proper Victorian watering hole which first opened in 1868, it was thankfully saved from closure in 2001 and is now a Grade II-listed building. With quizzes, happy-hour deals and a great Thai food menu, this is the sort of place you'd be very happy to have as your local. Take a seat at the front bar or explore the pub to find squishy sofas, comfy booths and a pretty conservatory. And keep an eye out for the resident cats.

51 Leverton Street, NW5 2NX
thepineapplepubnw5.com
@thepineapplepub
⊞ ⊘

Little Mercies

With exposed brickwork walls, pops of dark blue paint and plenty of tables for two or four, this understated neighbourhood bar in Crouch End is a great spot for a fun date or drinks with your mates. And when it comes to creative cocktails, Little Mercies is in a league of its own, serving up inventive twists on classics using its own flavoured spirits that are distilled in-house. That could be a Kiwi Gimlet with discarded Chardonnay vodka and fermented kiwi, or a sophisticated take on a Cosmopolitan with distilled Campari, lemon verbena pisco and lime leaves. Just as much care is given to its non-alcoholic cocktails, too. The bar's small plates menu changes, but might include dishes such as Mushroom Croquettes with Maple Sriracha, or a fusion take on Cacio e Pepe with szechuan pepper and German spätzle noodles. Can't get enough of the cocktails here? They sell bottled versions to take home, too.

20 Broadway Parade, N8 9DE
littlemercies.co.uk
@littlemercies

The Drapers Arms

The Drapers Arms

It's a great pub whatever the weather, but The Drapers Arms really comes into its own on a rainy day. Friendly staff, candle-lit tables and fireplaces all help to create a homely feel. Its classic horseshoe-shaped bar serves up a nice selection of beers and ales on tap and there's also an extensive wine list. The food menu adapts depending on the season, but whatever comes out of the kitchen, it's always mouth-wateringly tasty – there's usually a meaty, suet-crust pie, as well as joints of meat to share served on big platters (don't worry, veggies and pescatarians are well catered for too). If you just want a drink, plonk yourself on a sofa and peruse the selection of board games and Penguin classics.

44 Barnsbury Street, N1 1ER
thedrapersarms.com
@thedrapersarms

The High Cross

Homemade scotch eggs, a solid beer selection and a welcoming vibe – this Tottenham boozer is exactly what you'd expect from a really good pub. There's just one tiny thing that sets it apart from your average watering hole: it's housed in a former public toilet. Don't let that put you off – it's what makes this small-but-perfectly-formed pub so unique. If local football team Tottenham Hotspur FC are playing, it gets busy, so you might want to avoid it on match days. But otherwise, it's a lovely place to while away a rainy afternoon any day of the week. Look out for special deals on certain days, such as a pie and a pint for a tenner. Rude not to, right?

350 High Road, N17 9HT
@highcrosslondon

The Spaniards Inn

If you've ventured to Hampstead Heath for a walk and got caught
in a downpour, the nearby Spaniards Inn is a wonderful place to
take refuge. Built in 1585, this is a proper old-school boozer, with
wood panelling, traditional features and low ceilings (watch your
head on those). Named after the Spanish Ambassador to King
James I, this pub is steeped in history – Charles Dickens wrote
about it in *The Pickwick Papers* and legend has it that this is where
John Keats wrote 'Ode to a Nightingale'. There are also rumours
of ghost sightings (infamous highway robber Dick Turpin being
one of them), but don't let talk of the undead put you off. With
open fires, comfy sofas and lots of nooks and crannies to hole up
in, you'll be given a warm welcome at this classic London pub.

Spaniards Road, NW3 7JJ
thespaniardshampstead.co.uk
@thespaniardsinn

Kenwood House

Kenwood House

On the edge of picturesque Hampstead Heath sits Kenwood House, a grand stately home which dates back to the 17th century. It's a striking building with a long history, having been home to various aristocrats, including Judge Lord Mansfield, his great-niece Dido Belle (whose story inspired the 2013 film *Belle*) and Edward Guinness, who headed up his family's brewing business. The house is now run by English Heritage and you can dig into the building's past with a fascinating highlights tour (drop-in, no need to book ahead). Expect to see antique furniture, sculptures and jewellery, as well as artworks by the likes of Rembrandt and Reynolds. With its grand columns and carefully restored pastel blue and pink interiors, the Great Library is a real highlight. There's also a café, a kid's trail, a secondhand bookshop and gift shops.

Hampstead Lane, NW3 7JR
english-heritage.org.uk
@EHKenwood
☺ ✪

British Library

The Magna Carta. The notebooks of Leonardo da Vinci. Jane Austen's writing desk. Incredibly, you can see all of these things for free in the British Library's permanent exhibition. Aptly-named 'Treasures of the British Library', it's jam-packed with books, manuscripts and maps covering 2,000 years of history. The library also puts on other exhibitions and has a thought-provoking events programme. Of course, there's the actual library, too. You need to sign up for a free membership card if you want to get into the reading rooms, giving you access to a whopping 170 million items. If you want to pop into another important London literary location while you're in the area, London's long-running LGBTQ+ bookshop Gay's the Word is a short walk away and well worth a visit.

96 Euston Road, NW1 2DB
bl.uk
@britishlibrary
☺ ✪

Rowans Tenpin Bowl

It's hard to believe that a bowling alley could be described as 'legendary' but there really is nowhere else like Rowans. This north London institution is basically an indoor playground for people of all ages, with retro bowling alleys, karaoke booths, an arcade and pool tables, set across two floors. By day, it's the perfect place to take your kids or for a chilled bowling session with friends. Come evening, it transforms into a seriously fun place for a night out, with DJs playing pop and R&B classics and the bar serving up boozy slushies. Even if your bowling skills aren't up to much, you're guaranteed a good time.

10 Stroud Green Road, N4 2DF
rowans.co.uk
@rowansbowling
☺ 🏠

Screen on the Green

As the name suggests, this long-standing north London cinema has just one screen (and it's opposite Islington Green, in case you were wondering). One of the country's oldest cinemas, it first opened in 1913. Nearly 100 years later, it was taken over by swanky cinema chain The Everyman in 2008, but thankfully, it has retained its charm as well as its distinctive facade with a glowing red neon sign. In fact, the biggest change is that you can order food and drink to your seat. As well as the latest releases, its programme features Q&A events, special seasons (such as 90s or Horror) and National Theatre Live broadcasts.

83 Upper Street, N1 0NP
everymancinema.com
@everymanscreenonthegreen
☺ 🏠

Screen on the Green

Wellcome Collection

Did you know that doctors in 18th-century Britain thought that injecting tobacco smoke into a person's rectum would revive them from drowning? That's the sort of unusual trivia you'll come away with after a visit to the Wellcome Collection. Exploring connections between science, medicine, life and art, this Euston museum features just some of 19th-century pharmacist Sir Henry Wellcome's vast collection, which, as well as one of those questionable resuscitation kits, includes Napoleon's engraved toothbrush and Charles Darwin's skull-handled walking stick. The museum's intriguing permanent and temporary exhibitions look at how we feel and think about health. If you want to delve deeper into these topics, or find a quiet corner to read your own book, the reading room is a lovely spot that's filled with bean bags and comfy seats.

183 Euston Road, NW1 2BE
wellcomecollection.org
@wellcomecollection
☺ ✪

Coal Drops Yard

A swanky shopping quarter in a former Victorian coal depot, Coal Drops Yard was designed by Thomas Heatherwick (the architect behind the Olympic cauldron in the 2012 opening ceremony). It's a mix of well-established brands – Aesop, Cos, Paul Smith – alongside smaller independent businesses like Earl of East (a Hackney lifestyle store) and Walthamstow-based jeans manufacturer Blackhorse Lane Ateliers. Pick up serious chef knives at Kitchen Provisions, London-brewed craft beer at House of Cans and root through vinyl at Honest Jon's, a renowned record shop, which started in Notting Hill. Hit up Boutique by Shelter for vintage and designer fashion at decent prices (and to help raise money for the homeless charity it supports), or if you're caught off guard by rainy weather, pick up practical but stylish outdoorsy clothes at Rains and Outsiders Store. There are loads of places to eat and drink, too. Try the toasties at Morty & Bob's, head to Sons + Daughters for hefty sandwiches with creative fillings, or spice things up with Mexican food and margaritas at Casa Pastor.

Stable Street, N1C 4DQ
coaldropsyard.com
@coaldropsyard

Provisions

Provisions

Whether you're a cheese enthusiast looking to treat yourself or you're on the hunt for foodie gifts, Provisions will supply you with something delicious. This lovely shop works closely with artisan producers and stocks more than 100 cheeses and 120 wines. And that's not all – its shelves and fridges are loaded with craft beer, fresh bread, refillable wines on tap and deli bits such as chutneys, cured meats and top-quality olive oil. As well as its original branch on Holloway Road, there's a second location in Hackney. Both shops double up as wine bars (and there's a special sandwich menu at the Hackney store), so after you're done shopping, grab a seat and tuck in to some snacks and wine.

167 Holloway Road, N7 8LX
Other locations: Hackney
provisionslondon.co.uk
@provisionsldn

Flashback Islington

Go in search of second-hand vinyl at independent record shop Flashback. Established in 1997, the Islington branch is the original, but there are also outposts in Crouch End and Shoreditch. There's a good selection of new vinyl and CDs on the ground floor, but if you're keen to go digging for second-hand treasures, head to the basement, which is home to a vast range of used vinyl. If something piques your interest, you can give it a spin at one of the listening posts. With a collection that covers everything from jazz to hip hop, you're unlikely to leave empty-handed.

50 Essex Road, N1 8LR
Other locations: Crouch End, Shoreditch
flashback.co.uk
@flashbacklondon

Owl Bookshop

Yes, you can buy books on the internet, but local gems like Owl Bookshop will remind you why going to an actual shop is so much nicer. Open since 1974, this charming Kentish Town institution is well stocked with fiction, non-fiction, cookery, travel, poetry and more, while young bookworms will appreciate its extensive children's section. Authors regularly pop in, too – either to sign copies of their books or for in-store events. If you're looking for a gift, knowledgeable staff can offer suggestions and you can also pick up cute cards and wrapping paper. You might find it hard not to get something for yourself, too – and if you fancy flicking through your new purchases over a cuppa (or a pint), there are lots of cafés and pubs nearby.

207–209 Kentish Town Road, NW5 2JU
owlbookshop.co.uk
@owl.bookshop

W Martyn

You'll smell the freshly roasted coffee wafting out of this long-standing Muswell Hill grocery even before you've come through the door. But the impressive roasting machine in the shop window isn't the only draw here. Dating back to 1897, this place has been in the Martyn family for four generations. Stepping inside feels a bit like going back in time – in a good way. The layout hasn't ever changed and it still has its original counter. The walls are lined with shelves stacked with food and drink goodies made by independent producers. From jams and chutneys to sweet treats and even the shop's own loose leaf tea, it's ideal for picking up gifts that you won't find in big stores.

135 Muswell Hill Broadway, N10 3RS
wmartyn.co.uk
@wmartynmuswellhill

W Martyn

West

In the mood to learn about the world around you or appreciate some ancient artefacts? Get yourself to west London. Or more specifically, South Kensington, where many of the city's best museums – the V&A, the Science Museum and the Natural History Museum – are conveniently located in the same area. But world-class museums aren't the only thing this corner of the city has going for it. Pop into cute shops, cafés and restaurants in neighbourhoods like Chelsea, Kensington and Notting Hill (where you can admire the pretty pastel houses and pretend you're in a Richard Curtis film), or splash the cash in Knightsbridge at the vast department store that is Harrods.

Maître Choux

Lined up in neat rows and decorated with such precision, the pastries at Maître Choux are so pretty, you almost won't want to eat them. Almost. But with toppings that range from perfectly piped chocolate ganache to a pastel green Persian pistachio cream, you won't be able to hold off taking a bite for long. Specializing in sweet treats made with choux pastry, this place brings a modern approach to traditional French pâtisserie. There's a selection of different pastries on the menu, but the éclairs are the main attraction. Get a box to take away or find a seat in the café where the picture-perfect aesthetics continue with a wall of pink flowers.

15 Harrington Road, SW7 3ES
Other locations: Soho, Chelsea
maitrechoux.com
@maitrechoux
☺ ⊘

Milk Beach

Grey skies in London? Head to buzzy all-day restaurant Milk Beach for a taste of Aussie sunshine. This popular Queen's Park spot serves up colourful plates of food with an Antipodean influence – Smashed Avocado on Sourdough Toast topped with Confit Cherry Tomatoes and Feta, Sea Bream Tacos and a Yellowfin Tuna and Black Rice Poke Bowl. Oh, and you can get Vegemite on toast, obviously (don't even think about asking for Marmite). It's walk-ins only for brunch but you can book for dinner, as well as its wine-tasting nights. Milk Beach is a fun place to hang out any day of the week, but it's particularly lively on Saturday evenings when it hosts live music nights.

19–21 Lonsdale Road, NW6 6DH
Other locations: Soho
milkbeach.com
@milkbeachlondon

Ottolenghi

Israeli-born chef Yotam Ottolenghi is known for his imaginative Middle Eastern recipes and bringing ingredients like tahini, sumac and za'atar into people's kitchen cupboards. But if you don't fancy spending hours cooking, he also has his own restaurants where other people do the hard work for you. At Ottolenghi's delis, the counters are stacked high with vibrant salads, gorgeous cakes and massive piles of meringues. You will want to eat all of it. The Chelsea branch is one of the bigger ones and there are no reservations, so you should be able to turn up and get a table. The menu changes regularly but as well as the mouth-watering counter display, there are hot breakfast and lunch dishes (for breakfast, the shakshuka is always a winner). It's not a meat-free menu, but Ottolenghi does incredible things with vegetables that will convert even a diehard carnivore.

261 Pavilion Road, SW1X 0BP
Other locations: Notting Hill, Islington, Spitalfields, Marylebone
ottolenghi.co.uk
@ottolenghi_london

Ottolenghi

Petersham Nurseries Café and Teahouse

If the weather isn't up to much, Petersham Nurseries brings the best of the outdoors inside with lush foliage and beautiful flowers dotted around the space. As well as being a plant nursery and shop, there are two eateries, both dishing up seasonal food. The teahouse serves pastries, granola, hearty salads, pasta dishes and homemade cakes. There's also the café, which is actually more of a restaurant and has been awarded a Green Michelin Star for its commitment to sustainability (it's more upmarket than the teahouse and prices reflect that – expect to pay at least £80 for a three-course set menu, including a bellini). If you're not ready to leave after eating, you can browse the huge plant selection and the lifestyle and homeware shop. You could happily spend hours here.

Church Lane, off Petersham Road, TW10 7AB
Other locations: Covent Garden
petershamnurseries.com
@petershamnurseries

Kricket

Having started out with a 20-seater space in a shipping container in Brixton, Kricket has gone from strength to strength since it launched in 2015. It now has restaurants in Brixton (in a bigger space, thankfully), Soho and White City. The west London site is the biggest, making it your best bet for a walk-in on a rainy day (although you can book, too). Its Indian-inspired menu features creative uses of spices and contemporary takes on classic dishes, such as Samphire Pakoras. Whatever you do, get the Keralan Fried Chicken – it's crispy, delicious and served with a moreish curry leaf mayonnaise. There's plenty to get excited about on the drinks menu too – the Dark Matter cocktail with green chilli rum and mango, for instance, or the house beer, which has been specially crafted to complement the food.

101 Wood Lane, W12 7FR
Other locations: Soho, Brixton
kricket.co.uk
@kricketlondon
🏛

The Churchill Arms

Over the festive season, this Kensington drinking spot is often described as the city's most Christmassy pub. That's down to its impressive display, which involves covering the building's exterior in real Christmas trees and hundreds of sparkling lights. But it's worth a visit all year round, as those festive firs are replaced with pretty window boxes (the pub has even won awards from the Chelsea Flower Show). The foliage continues inside, with hanging plants and flower pots alongside antique trinkets hanging from the ceiling. Minimalist, it is not. Built in 1750, it was frequented by Winston Churchill's grandparents in the 1800s. It was renamed The Churchill Arms after World War II, which explains the vast collection of memorabilia relating to the wartime Prime Minister. These days, it's run by nearby Fuller's brewery, so expect decent ales on tap alongside its menu of tasty Thai food.

119 Kensington Church Street, W8 7LN
churchillarmskensington.co.uk
@churchillarmsw8

The Distillery

In a four-storey townhouse on Portobello Road, The Distillery is a one-stop shop for all your drinking needs. It has two bars, a working distillery and hosts workshops where you can make your own gin or whiskey. If you have one too many cocktails, it even has three swanky hotel rooms on the top floor. The Resting Room bar specializes in G&Ts made with different varieties of The Distillery's Portobello Road Gin, as well as Martinis and creative cocktails (like the Paddington Bear's Marmalade Sandwich, sprinkled with 'toast dust'). Upstairs is The Malt Floor bar, where the drinks menu is focused on whiskey from around the world. You can just pop in for a drink, but if you want to stay over, or try a boozy experience (there's gin-making, whiskey-making, tequila tasting and a James Bond-themed extravaganza), you'll need to book ahead.

186 Portobello Road, W11 1LA
the-distillery.london
@distilleryldn

The Harwood Arms

There's no shortage of great boozers in the capital, but there's only one Michelin-starred pub – and that's The Harwood Arms. It's no surprise, then, that the food here is not your average pub grub. On a quiet street in Fulham, this popular spot celebrates British produce, focusing on game and foraged food. It has an extensive list of interesting wines, too. Despite its Michelin-star status, the atmosphere isn't stuffy and prices aren't extortionate (there's a three-course set menu for £65). You'll need to book a few weeks ahead to get a table for food, especially if you want to sample the cracking Sunday roasts, but you can pop in for a drink at the bar without a reservation. You can't order from the main food menu at the bar but you can (and definitely should) get a Venison Scotch Egg as a snack to go with your tipple.

Walham Grove, SW6 1QP
harwoodarms.com
@theharwoodarms
⊞

The Harwood Arms

The Dove

It's pretty rare to find a pub with a Guinness World Record, but that's the case at this riverside watering hole in Hammersmith. The Dove's claim to fame? It's home to the smallest public bar room in the UK. The space in question is to the right of the bar, through an entrance you might easily miss. But inquisitive punters will find a secret spot that seats two people (maybe three, at a push). It's a fun quirk, but thankfully there's plenty of seating in the main pub, decked out with squishy armchairs and a fireplace for colder days. This 17th-century boozer is also a place of legend – it's said that poet James Thomson wrote 'Rule Britannia' here, while King Charles II allegedly used it as a meeting point for secret rendezvous with his mistress Nell Gwynne. Something to ponder as you sip your pint.

19 Upper Mall, W6 9TA
dovehammersmith.co.uk
@the_dove_hammersmith

Trailer Happiness

No matter what the weather is doing, you'll find tropical vibes at Trailer Happiness in Notting Hill. The cocktails are heavy on the rum at this award-winning, tiki-themed basement bar, with an extensive menu full of classic drinks (Mai Thai, Margarita) and more unusual creations (an Espresso Martiki made with spiced rum and Tia Maria liqueur). The sharing cocktails are a highlight, especially the Zombie – a heady mix of the bar's own five-rum blend, absinthe and two types of liqueur. Served in a dramatic fashion, it's poured into a mini barbecue grill and set alight. Need some sustenance to balance out all that booze? Thankfully, there's food, too – patties, chicken wings and fragrant curries served with roti are all on offer. Who needs actual sunshine?

177 Portobello Road, W11 2DY
trailerh.com
@trailerh

Electric Cinema

If you're after something a bit more luxe than your bog-standard seat at a multiplex, head to Electric Cinema, which is kitted out with comfy armchairs, sofas and, best of all... *beds*. Yes, really. They stop short at providing duvets (you're not there to sleep, after all) but you can expect cushions and blankets on the red velvet-covered double beds that line the front row. And with food and drink available to order to your seat (or bed), this is definitely a cut above your average cinema experience. Its Notting Hill location is one of London's oldest cinemas, which has been lovingly restored and there's also a newer branch in White City at the former home of the BBC.

191 Portobello Road, W11 2ED
Other locations: White City
electriccinema.co.uk
@electriccinemas
☺ 🏢

Science Museum

Whether you're a science whizz or your knowledge of the periodic table is a little sketchy, the Science Museum aims to make learning about scientific, technological and medical developments fun and engaging for all ages. There are 15,000 objects across seven floors to explore, but highlights include the spacecraft that Tim Peake travelled to the International Space Station in, a reconstruction of Crick and Watson's DNA model and a piece of the actual moon. Kids will love the Wonderlab (but be aware you'll need to pay for entry), where they can interact with live lightning demonstrations, a massive slide and a rotating model of the solar system. Elsewhere, you can have a go on the Red Arrow jet simulator or watch a film in the IMAX cinema. It's a great place to learn without having to go anywhere near a boring textbook.

Exhibition Road, SW7 2DD
sciencemuseum.org.uk
@sciencemuseum
☺ ✩

Natural History Museum

Natural History Museum

Ever wanted to see the skeleton of a Stegosaurus? Or how about the pigeons Charles Darwin bred in his garden? These are just a couple of the 80 million specimens the Natural History Museum has in its staggeringly expansive collection covering 4.5 billion years of natural history (for obvious reasons, not everything is on display at one time). Divided into different coloured zones, visitors can get up close to creepy crawlies, fossils going back millions of years, a 25-metre blue whale and so much more. The animatronic dinos are always a big hit with kids and experiencing the shake of the famous earthquake simulator is practically a London rite of passage. There's even an audio tour narrated by none other than national treasure Sir David Attenborough. As well as the vast permanent displays, there are thought-provoking temporary exhibitions, too. You'll leave feeling in awe of the natural wonders of our planet.

Cromwell Road, SW7 5BD
nhm.ac.uk
@natural_history_museum
☺ ✪

Design Museum

The Design Museum is the new kid on the block compared to some of the other South Kensington institutions. Founded by the late Sir Terence Conran, a design legend, it opened in 1989 in a former banana warehouse along the Thames. In 2016, it relocated to a bigger space in west London, which is a spectacular building in itself, even before you take a look at what's inside. The museum showcases how design and innovation have shaped our world, covering fashion, furniture and technology. 'Designer, Maker, User' is its permanent (and free) exhibition, featuring nearly 1,000 items from the world of modern design, including a prototype for a London tube train, a London 2012 Olympic Torch and a Sony Walkman. Previous temporary shows have focused on topics ranging from Stanley Kubrick to football to electronic music.

224–238 Kensington High Street, W8 6AG
designmuseum.org
@designmuseum
☺ ✪

V&A

What do Charles Dickens' pen case, Mick Jagger's jumpsuit and Henry VIII's desk have in common? They're all part of the V&A Museum's magnificent collection, which spans 5,000 years of art and design. First established in 1852 in Pall Mall, it was originally called the slightly less catchy 'Museum of Manufactures'. It eventually moved to Brompton, which the museum authorities renamed 'South Kensington' to make it sound more fashionable. It became the Victoria and Albert Museum in 1899, when Queen Victoria laid the foundation stone of one of its new buildings. Decades later, it's still one of the world's top museums. It hosts blockbuster temporary shows alongside a vast permanent collection that's split into themed rooms featuring art, photography, sculpture, metalwork, textiles, fashion and lots more. The events programme includes kids' activities, free tours and monthly 'late' events. Don't miss the chance for a pit stop in the main café – it was the world's first museum café and it's a stunning setting for a cuppa.

Cromwell Road, SW7 2RL
vam.ac.uk
@vamuseum
☺ ✪

Harrods

With its name (and the entire building) all lit up in twinkling lights, this massive department store makes quite an impression before you've even walked through its doors. Harrods is all about luxury, so don't expect to leave here with a bargain, but it's fascinating to visit even if you don't want to splash the cash. The food hall is a real feast for the eyes (and possibly your stomach too, as not *everything* is wildly expensive here) – from exquisite pâtisserie to a vast cheese counter. Listen out for the bell being rung in the bakery – it means they're putting freshly baked goods out. If you can tear yourself away from the food hall, there's plenty more to explore – the grand beauty and perfume halls, fashion and homeware, for a start. Those with kids should head to the fourth floor for toys and a Harry Potter-themed section (there's even a toy concierge, if you can believe it), while fashion-forward adults might prefer to get lost in the equally magical Shoe Heaven.

87–135 Brompton Road, SW1X 7XL
harrods.com
@harrods

Next Door Records

Whether you're a vinyl enthusiast or a wine connoisseur (or both), Next Door Records has something for you. That's because this Shepherd's Bush spot is a real crowd pleaser – a record shop that also sells natural wine and local beer. On top of that, it serves coffee, has a bar and hosts regular events including gigs, DJ sets, film screenings and supper clubs. A love of vinyl is at the heart of it all – and you'll find a mix of new and vintage records across a variety of genres, which you can dig into at one of the listening stations. Check out its website for the latest goings-on at this west London gem that's way more than just a shop.

304 Uxbridge Road, W12 7LJ
nextdoorrecords.co.uk
@nextdoorrecords_

Rough Trade West

Rough Trade West

This famous Notting Hill record shop has a rich history. Founded by Geoff Travis in 1976, Rough Trade had an anti-establishment and egalitarian ethos (all staff were paid the same), meaning it was well placed to champion the burgeoning punk movement. Soon, the likes of The Ramones and Talking Heads were doing in-store performances. Eventually, it launched its own independent label, Rough Trade Records. But in 1982, the business got into trouble and the shop's three employees bought it and relocated to Talbot Road. It's still there today and sells much more than punk records – genres range from electronica to jazz and everything in between. There's a bigger branch of Rough Trade in east London at Old Truman Brewery, which is worth a visit, but with its punk posters and records by The Clash on the walls, there's a certain charm about the Notting Hill shop.

130 Talbot Road, W11 1JA
Other locations: Brick Lane
roughtrade.com
@roughtradewest

Nomad Books

If you just happen to walk past this indie bookshop on Fulham Road, you'd likely be drawn in by the ever-changing and always eye-catching window displays. Step inside to explore a huge range of books, from hot new bestsellers to cookbooks to a selection of French titles. The main room is full of recommendations, but those with kids should head straight to the brilliant children's section, which is well stocked with engaging reads for all ages and comfy sofas to curl up on. The shop regularly hosts talks and book signing events, as well as free, drop-in storytime sessions for kids, where authors bring their books to life. If you're not sure where to start, the staff are very happy to talk about all things book-related.

781 Fulham Road, SW6 5HA
nomadbooks.co.uk
@nomad_books
☺

Alfie's Antique Market

In a striking Art Deco building with four floors of antiques and vintage items, Alfie's Antique Market is one of London's best places for secondhand shopping. Before it opened as Alfie's in 1976, the space was home to a department store called Jordan's for nearly a century. Now, the 30,000-square-foot building is filled with around 100 dealers whose wares include furniture, jewellery, clothes and homeware. It's a treasure trove for everything from mid-century furniture to antique watches. Even if you just want to gawp at expensive pieces you'll never actually buy, it's a great spot to mooch around. And if you need a break from retail therapy, there's a rooftop café, which thankfully has indoor space for less sunny days.

13–25 Church Street, NW8 8DT
alfiesantiques.com
@alfiesantiques

South

There are plenty of reasons to head south of the river – incredible food, creative cocktails and brilliant culture are just a few of them. Neighbourhoods like Brixton, Peckham and Camberwell have a real Afro-Caribbean influence as many of the Windrush generation moved to these areas in the 1970s. Elsewhere, there's the Bermondsey Beer Mile (a stretch of artisan breweries and taprooms), the railway arches of Deptford (now transformed into shops, cafés and bars) and the residential neighbourhoods of Dulwich and Forest Hill. While the tube does go to places like Brixton and Bermondsey, south London is generally better served by buses, the DLR, the Overground and National Rail trains.

Roti King

Roti King

Since it first opened in 2014 on a quiet, unassuming backstreet in Euston, Malaysian restaurant Roti King has developed a cult following. The only downside of its success is that punters often have to queue around the block to get in, which is why it's excellent news that there's now a second, much bigger site across the river at Battersea Power Station. There's a selection of noodle and rice dishes but really, you're here for one thing: the Roti Canai (Malaysian flatbread), which is flakey, buttery and indescribably delicious. Try a filled roti stuffed with cheese or meat, or have it unadulterated and use it to scoop up a flavourful kari (options include dahl, chicken, mutton and fish). Looking to get your fix elsewhere? Try your luck in Euston, or head to its food hall spin-off stall Gopal's Corner at Market Halls in Canary Wharf, Victoria and on Oxford Street. Whatever dish you order on the menu, you'll get change from a tenner. This is affordable comfort food at its finest.

**Battersea Power Station,
16 Arches Lane, SW11 8AB
Other locations: Euston, and at
Market Halls' Canary Wharf, Victoria
and Oxford Street branches
rotiking.com
@rotikinguk**

Garden Museum Café

Museum cafés aren't usually a destination in their own right, but the Garden Museum Café is an exception. First opened in the 1970s, the museum is housed in an atmospheric old church which was saved from demolition. The café is a newer addition, opened in 2017 after a refurbishment. It's built around the museum's plant-filled courtyard, with full-length glass windows allowing you to admire the foliage. As is fitting for a place that celebrates greenery, the menu is full of fresh flavours made with seasonal British produce. Dishes change weekly, if not daily. It's a great spot for a long, leisurely lunch, or for a cup of tea and homemade cake. A meal here will set you back more than at your average museum café (mains can be around the £20 mark), but that's down to the care that goes into the cooking and ingredients. You can go to the café without visiting the museum, but green-fingered folks may want to dig into its collection showcasing the history of British gardens.

**5 Lambeth Palace Road, SE1 7LB
gardenmuseum.org.uk
@gardenmuseumcafe**

Larry's

With a sparkling disco ball in the ceiling, bright orange tables and green chairs, it's clear from the moment you arrive at Larry's that this place is a lot of fun. Taking inspiration from across the Atlantic, it has an American diner aesthetic and serves dishes that draw on the melting pot of cuisines (Chinese, Italian, Jewish) that you'd find in New York. The menu is handwritten on a backlit whiteboard, as it changes regularly, but the food is always creative and really, really tasty – ranging from punchy pasta dishes to toasties stuffed with delicious things and oozing cheese. The hash browns served with fermented chilli mayonnaise are always on the menu and you should definitely order them. Larry's also has a sister restaurant next door called Levan, which serves up equally good, slightly fancier food.

Unit 5, 12–16 Blenheim Grove, SE15 4QL
Other locations: Levan, Peckham
larryspeckham.co.uk
@larryspeckham
☺ 🏦

M.Manze

Food trends come and go in London, but pie-and-mash shops have been around since the 19th century. Many of them have closed down, but M.Manze is one of the oldest – and it's still going strong. It's named after Michele Manze, an Italian immigrant whose parents moved to Bermondsey in the late 1800s. At one point, the Manze family had 14 pie-and-mash shops in the capital, but the Tower Bridge branch was the first, dating back to 1902. Serving up reasonably-priced pie, mash, liquor and eels, the menu is pretty much the same as it always was. As is tradition, there's just one flavour of pie (minced beef), although there is now a vegan option made with soya mince. The 'liquor' has nothing to do with booze – it's a traditional parsley sauce and whatever you do, don't call it gravy.

87 Tower Bridge Road, SE1 4TW
Other locations: Peckham, Sutton
manze.co.uk
@manzespieandmash

Mercato Metropolitano

Whatever you're in the mood to eat, you'll be spoilt for choice at Mercato Metropolitano. Housed in a previously abandoned paper factory, this covered food market in Elephant & Castle has more than 40 traders. The vibe here is casual and relaxed – grab a seat at one of the communal tables and then comes the hard part: deciding what to eat. Neapolitan pizza, Vietnamese noodles and jerk chicken are just some of the things you can sample. The market also hosts events, including live music, wine and jazz nights and pop-up markets showcasing independent makers. Its Elephant & Castle market is the original site, but it has expanded in recent years, with a second massive market in an atmospheric old church in Mayfair with beautiful stained glass windows. It also has smaller spots in Canary Wharf and Elephant Park (a development in Elephant & Castle).

42 Newington Causeway, SE1 6DR
Other locations: Canary Wharf,
Elephant Park, Mayfair
mercatometropolitano.com
@mercatometropolitano

Brew By Numbers

Don't get the wrong idea about this brewery's name – there's nothing formulaic about the beers that Brew By Numbers produce (but each one is given a number as well as a name). In an old railway arch in Bermondsey, this taproom offers the chance to sip super-fresh beer and the latest concoctions that the BBNo crew have been brewing. A no-frills space filled with beer barrels and trestle tables, this place is part of the unofficial Bermondsey Beer Mile – a stretch of taprooms and bottle shops that have set up shop within the railway arches and sprawling estates in this area. The brewery has also opened a second, much bigger location in an old warehouse in Greenwich's Morden Wharf, where you can tuck into wood-fired pizza alongside more fresh beer.

79 Enid St, SE16 3RA
Other locations: Greenwich
bbno.co
@brewbynumbers

The Camberwell Arms

From the outside, with its dark green exterior, gold letter signage and hanging baskets, The Camberwell Arms looks like your typical London local. But inside, you won't find sticky carpets or mediocre bottles of pinot grigio behind the bar. Instead, the decor here is classy and understated. As for drinks, there are natural wines, decent beers and cocktails that range from the classic (Negroni, Martini) to the more unusual (Amontillado Sherry and Tonic). The pub's kitchen is all about seasonal cooking and the menu will make your mouth water as you scan through it. If you're just after a drink, grab a seat in the front bar and order some small plates if you get peckish. If you're keen to have dinner or try one of the pub's award-winning Sunday roasts, it's best to book a table in the dining room.

65 Camberwell Church Street, SE5 8TR
thecamberwellarms.co.uk
@thecamberwellarms

Little Nan's Bar

Leopard print cushions, vintage teacups, a bust of 'Eastenders' character Pat Butcher... the decor at Little Nan's Bar is an explosion of 80s kitsch. But the theme wasn't a calculated marketing ploy – owner Tristan Scutt created this bar in honour of his late nan Jojo, who lived to the ripe old age of 104. In fact, lots of the bar's furniture and trinkets were passed down from her. The OTT vibes continue on the menus, a dizzying selection of hand-written and collaged lists of cocktails and dishes that don't take themselves too seriously (anyone for Disco Fries and a Porn Star Nan?). Whether you come for a boozy brunch, afternoon tea or a night of cocktails in teacups, this place is a real joy.

Arches 13–15, Deptford Market Yard,
SE8 4BX
littlenans.co.uk
@littlenansbar
☺

Forza Wine

The dilemma: you want to experience a rooftop bar in London, but... it's raining. The solution? Forza Wine. This sky-high spot in Peckham has all weather covered. If the skies clear up, there's an outdoor terrace, but for a rain-friendly rooftop experience, the indoor space with glass doors and full-length windows means you can still gaze at the city's skyline. But the views aren't the only draw. The bar is a sister site to ace Italian restaurant Forza Win, so expect food and drink with an Italian feel. Obviously there's a good wine selection (the clue's in the name), but don't miss the creative cocktails, too (Negroni Sour, Watermelon Martini). And the 'bar snacks' are much more exciting (and substantial) than a bowl of salted peanuts – order a selection and you've got dinner sorted.

The Rooftop, 133A Rye Lane, SE15 4BQ
forzawine.com
@forzawine

Kanpai London Sake Brewery & Taproom

London isn't short of craft beer breweries, but on a former industrial estate in Peckham, you'll find something a little more unusual. Covered in a brightly coloured graffiti mural, you can't miss Kanpai. This is the UK's first sake brewery – and it brews its goods right here in SE15. For the unfamiliar, sake is a Japanese alcoholic drink made with fermented rice and Kanpai means 'cheers' or 'dry your cup' in Japanese – which you'll be able to do as much as you like thanks to the brewery's on-site taproom. Whether you've never tried sake or you're obsessed with the stuff, there are lots of different varieties on offer, as well as Japanese beer, whiskey and liqueurs. You can also grab tasty Japanese dishes from Okan, the street food stall opposite. If you're keen to learn more about sake and how it's made, they offer tours, which need to be booked in advance.

Unit 2A–2 Copeland Park,
133 Copeland Road, SE15 3SN
kanpai.london
@kanpailondon

Horniman Museum & Gardens

There's no shortage of things to see at this kid-friendly museum in Forest Hill, but let's start with one of its biggest and most popular exhibits: a giant stuffed walrus. This one-ton specimen has been part of the museum's collection since 1901 and these days, it even has its own Twitter account. Once you're done admiring the overstuffed walrus (the Victorian taxidermists thought they needed to get all the wrinkles out of its skin), explore the rest of the natural history collection which includes fossils, dried and pressed plants, birds' eggs and, yes, more taxidermy. You'll also find art, textiles and archaeological materials from around the world. There are some living animals here too – you have to pay to visit the butterfly house, a tropical indoor garden filled with free-flying butterflies and moths, as well as the aquarium, but both are worth checking out.

100 London Road, SE23 3PQ
horniman.ac.uk
@hornimanmuseumgardens
☺ ✿

Ritzy Cinema

This south London cinema is a much-loved Brixton institution, but it wasn't always this way. One of London's oldest picture houses, it first opened in 1911 as The Electric Pavilion. Back then, it was known as the 'flea pit' and thought of as the scruffy relation of the nearby Palladium (which is now performance venue Electric Brixton). Having escaped demolition in the 1970s, the cinema has since been spruced up. It now has five screens and a bar, while its Edwardian exterior and auditorium have been restored to show off this early example of cinema architecture. It's also known for its eye-catching readograph sign on the front of the building, which came from an abandoned cinema in Hammersmith. Its programme ranges from blockbuster hits to niche arthouse flicks, while Upstairs at Ritzy hosts stand-up comedy, live music and open mic nights.

Brixton Oval, Coldharbour Lane, SW2 1JG
picturehouses.com
@ritzy_cinema
☺ 🎬

Royal Observatory

Ever wondered what Greenwich Mean Time actually means? Learn all about it at the Royal Observatory. Established in the 17th century by Charles II and designed by renowned architect Christopher Wren (the brains behind St Paul's Cathedral), the Royal Observatory was set up to study astronomy in order to get a better understanding of the world and help navigate the seas. It's home to Christopher Wren's Octagon Room, designed to give astronomers an uninterrupted view of the sky at night, a 28-inch Great Equatorial Telescope – the largest of its kind in the UK – and a collection of historical and ground-breaking clocks. But it's not all about the concept of time. Space fans will love the Astronomy Centre, where you can admire a 4.5-billion-year-old meteorite, while the Peter Harrison Planetarium hosts shows that cater to kids, as well as more in-depth astrology. The Observatory is part of the Royal Museums Greenwich, which also includes the nearby National Maritime Museum and the Queen's House (an architectural gem filled with art), if you want to make a day of it.

Blackheath Avenue, SE10 8XJ
rmg.co.uk
@royalmuseumsgreenwich

Eltham Palace

A dedicated map room, a wartime basement bunker and quarters designed specifically for a pet lemur called Mahjong – some of the details of Eltham Palace sound made up (but it's all true, honest). Set within 19 acres of beautiful grounds, this English Heritage-run property in the suburbs of Greenwich is where medieval meets Art Deco. Built for Edward IV in the 1470s, the Tudor palace (which has its own moat, naturally) houses the Great Hall with its impressive open timber oak roof. The palace was pretty run down when millionaires Stephen and Virginia Courtauld decided to make it their home in the 1930s, restoring the Great Hall and adding an Art Deco mansion extension. With its pleasingly geometric shapes and wood-panelled walls, the entrance hall looks like something out of a Wes Anderson film, while the luxurious bathroom lined with gold mosaic tiles and onyx will give you serious loo envy.

Court Yard, SE9 5QE
english-heritage.org.uk
@ElthamPalace

Eltham Palace

Dulwich Picture Gallery

Fun fact: Dulwich Picture Gallery was the world's first purpose-built public art gallery. And it shows – the building is a thing of beauty, with arch-shaped doorways creating a sense of endless space, as well as glass roof-lanterns to let in natural light. It opened in 1817 and was designed by architect and collector St John Soane. He not only designed the gallery to house the artworks which belonged to collectors Francis Bourgeois and Noël Desenfans, but also built a mausoleum so that they could be buried within the gallery. As well as its interesting quirks, the gallery has a great collection of Old Master paintings by the likes of Rembrandt and Poussin. Look out for temporary exhibitions, talks that dig deeper into the artworks and family-friendly activities and trails.

Gallery Road, SE21 7AD
dulwichpicturegallery.org.uk
@dulwichgallery

Borough Market

Huge slabs of mortadella, tanks of fresh crabs, pungent cheeses... As you walk into the culinary hotspot that is Borough Market, it's impossible not to feel hungry. In fact, if you're coming to this iconic covered market, it's probably a good idea to have a light breakfast, because you're going to want to eat everything. The market has been here in some form since 1756. It was once a wholesale market for greengrocers but now there are more than 100 street food stalls, restaurants, wine bars, delis, fishmongers, cheesemongers and specialist food traders alongside the fruit and veg sellers. Need to satiate your appetite immediately? The food stalls offer something for all tastes, including massive pans of risotto, fresh oysters and falafel wraps. Oh, and if you spy The Ginger Pig's hefty sausage rolls or Bread Ahead's brilliant doughnuts, snap 'em up. You won't regret it.

8 Southwark Street, SE1 1TL
boroughmarket.org.uk
@boroughmarket

Northcote Road Antiques Market

At first glance, this Battersea antique shop looks pretty tiny – but head inside and you'll discover an Aladdin's cave of secondhand treasures. Set over two floors, there are more than 30 dealers selling vintage and antique wares, ranging from grand wooden furniture to dinky little trinkets. Art Deco lamps, vintage silverware and pretty antique cups and saucers are just some of the things you might end up bringing home with you – even if you thought you were just there to 'window shop'. It's crammed with unique items and there's a lot to see, making it an ideal place to explore when you're hiding out from the rain.

155A Northcote Road, SW11 6QB
northcoteroadantiques.co.uk
@NorthcoteRd

Brixton Village

This market in south London is actually two markets – now known collectively as Brixton Village, Market Row is on one side of Atlantic Road and Brixton Village is on the other. Both markets are covered – and with more than 100 traders, there's no danger of getting bored here. You'll find everything from unique reads for children at inclusive bookstore Round Table Books to ethically-sourced homeware and gifts from Rachel and Malika's. Elsewhere, there are butchers and fishmongers, grocery stalls specializing in Caribbean food and local institutions like First Choice Bakers for Jamaican patties. Fancy a sit-down meal? Options range from ever-reliable small chains (Franco Manco and Honest Burgers both started in Brixton and have spread across the city) to places unique to Brixton, including vibrant West African restaurant Chishuru or Fish, Wings and Tings for unbeatable cod fish fritters.

Coldharbour Lane, SW9 8PS
brixtonvillage.com
@brixton.village
☺

Dark Sugars Cocoa House

Dark Sugars Cocoa House

The smell of chocolate hits you as soon as you set foot in this cocoa lovers' paradise. Having started as a market stall selling two types of truffles, Dark Sugars' offering has vastly expanded over the years, with a shop on Brick Lane, its flagship shop and an ice cream shop (both in Greenwich). The store in Greenwich is a mecca for all things chocolate. Bowls and platters are piled high with truffles in all kinds of flavours – limoncello, hazelnut praline and pistachio – while its origin chocolate bar range showcases the lesser-known cocoa-growing countries. On a cold day, make a beeline for its hot chocolate counter, serving more than 20 flavours of velvety goodness topped with massive shards of chocolate. Want something stronger? There's also a 'choctail' bar serving chocolate cocktails.

9 Nelson Road, SE10 9JB
Other locations: Brick Lane
darksugars.co.uk
@darksugars

Forest

If you like the idea of filling your house with luscious foliage, but can't ever manage to keep your plants alive, the green-fingered folk at Forest are on hand to help. In a railway arch in Deptford, this shop specializes in easy-to-care-for plants, so you might actually have a fighting chance of not killing off your purchases. There's a second branch in East Dulwich and both shops sell chic homeware. They'll even help you pick out a pot to complement your plant. The Deptford store hosts monthly workshops where you can learn everything from flower arranging to candle-making. With plants hanging from the ceiling and shelves lined with cacti and succulents, it's a lovely spot to get immersed in greenery if you don't feel like braving the city's parks in the rain.

Arch 4, Deptford Market Yard, SE8 4NS
Other locations: East Dulwich
forest.london
@forest_london
☺

East

Many people associate east London with Shoreditch, an area known for being covered in street art and the place where street food took off in the capital. And while there's a lot to do there, it's not the only part worth visiting. There's the East End, which includes Whitechapel with its contemporary art gallery, Spitalfields and its famed covered market and Brick Lane – a bustling stretch of curry houses and cool shops (it's a great spot for vintage shopping). While in neighbourhoods like Dalston, Clapton and Hackney, you'll be spoilt for choice when it comes to coffee shops, cafés, pubs, bars and restaurants. This area has a rich past – learn more about it at Dalston's intriguing Museum of the Home or go further east to discover the Museum of London Docklands, which digs into London's history as a port.

Pophams

Crispy bacon, flaky pastry, drizzles of maple syrup – the sweet and savoury Bacon and Maple Syrup Pastry at Pophams is legendary. In fact, all the pastries at this brilliant bakery will have you drooling. The Marmite, Schlossberger Cheese and Spring Onion Pastry is another classic, but it also serves more 'conventional' croissants (regular, chocolate, almond), alongside ever-changing seasonal specials. You can get pastries for breakfast and toasties for lunch at its three cafés, but the London Fields spot has the added bonus of serving up fresh pasta dishes by night (the menu varies, but think: Ravioli stuffed with Beetroot and Gorgonzola or Braised Rabbit Cannelloni). Pophams is walk-ins only, except for the pasta nights, which you might want to book ahead.

197 Richmond Road, E8 3NJ
Other locations: Islington, Victoria Park
pophamsbakery.com
@pophamsbakery

Manteca

Manteca

Salami and mortadella cured in-house, hand-rolled fresh pasta, juicy cuts of meat cooked in a wood-fired oven... Manteca does not do things by half. With a focus on Italian-inspired dishes and nose-to-tail cooking, the menu at this lively Shoreditch restaurant changes regularly. There are some signature dishes which often appear, though – the Pig Skin Ragù, a bowl of rich, meaty sauce, topped with deep-fried pig skin that looks like a giant Quaver (sounds weird, tastes delicious), or fresh pasta in a silky smooth crab Cacio e Pepe sauce. Prices vary depending on what you get – expect to spend more if you go big on the grilled meat dishes, rather than the pasta. Set over two floors, there's an open kitchen on the ground floor so you can see the chefs at work, while the glass-panelled hanging room for the restaurant's in-house butchery and salumi is downstairs. Kick off your meal with an aperitif before sampling the wine selection, which includes some great options on tap.

49–51 Curtain Road, EC2A 3PT
mantecarestaurant.co.uk
@manteca_london

My Neighbours the Dumplings

There are no prizes for guessing what My Neighbours the Dumplings specializes in. But dumplings aren't the only thing on the menu at this independent eatery in Clapton. As well as freshly made Dim Sum and Potstickers, expect dishes such as Smacked Cucumber, Buttermilk Chicken Wings, Marinated Silken Tofu and a selection of specials. The food is designed for sharing and you'll be given a pencil with your menu to mark up which dishes you want and how many (tip: you'll almost definitely want to order an extra portion of the Pork and Prawn Dumplings). There's an interesting drinks list too, which ranges from sake and cocktails to specialist teas. You can book ahead but they also accept walk-ins.

165 Lower Clapton Road, E5 8EQ
Other locations: Victoria Park
myneighboursthedumplings.com
@myneighboursthedumplings

Draughts

Playing Monopoly is a classic rainy day activity, but if you really want to up your game, head to Draughts – a board game café with more than 1,000 unique games in its collection. Housed in a former pie-and-mash shop with Art Deco tiles and stained glass windows, its east London branch is full of character. It's also massive – there are seven different rooms with cosy sofas and armchairs, special board game-playing tables (they have a shelf below the table top) and even a full-sized shuffleboard table. There's a one-off payment, which gets you access to all the games – from classics like Cluedo (and yes, Monopoly) to newer games such as Ticket to Ride and Catan. Not sure what to go for? There's a handy sticker guide which indicates the skill level needed. If all that competitiveness tires you out, its menu of small plates, tacos and burgers, as well as craft beer, cocktails and wine, will help you refuel.

41 Kingsland High Street, E8 2JS
Other locations: Waterloo
draughtslondon.com
@draughtslondon
☺ 🏛

Koya Ko

Rainy days call for steaming hot bowls of udon noodle soup – and you'll find some of the city's best at Koya. There are branches in the City and Soho, but Koya Ko in Hackney is the cooler, more casual sister site. What sets Koya apart is the quality of its ingredients – both the udon noodles and the dashi (a Japanese stock that forms the basis of its soups) are made fresh every day. With these, Koya creates comforting dishes – from the traditional (Pork and Ginger Miso Soup) to the more unusual (an English breakfast-inspired udon with raw egg, bacon and butter soy mushrooms). Alongside super-fresh udon, there's also a range of rice dishes and sides. Koya Ko has a special offering for kids, too – they've even got child-friendly chopsticks.

10 Broadway Market Mews, E8 4TS
Other locations: City, Soho
koya.co.uk
@koyalondon
 ☺ ✓

Three Sheets

With a name that takes inspiration from the phrase 'three sheets to the wind', you'd be forgiven for thinking that this Dalston bar is all about getting drunk. Obviously, that's not out of the question, but the focus at Three Sheets is classic cocktails done really well and often with a unique twist. The menu is divided into three sections, which increase in flavour intensity as they go on (one sheet, two sheets, three sheets). Whatever you choose, you're in safe hands – this place is frequently awarded a spot on The World's 50 Best Bars list – and for good reason. The menu changes but the French 75, a mix of carbonated gin, lemon, Moscato and orange flower that slips down very easily, is thankfully a permanent fixture. If you get a taste for the cocktails, you can buy bottled versions from Shop Cuvée in Finsbury Park – a spin-off from sister site Top Cuvée that's also worth checking out.

510B Kingsland Road, London E8 4AE
threesheets-bar.com
@threesheetslondon

Sager + Wilde

Candle-lit tables, excellent wine and cheese toasties – Hackney wine bar Sager + Wilde is a very good place to weather a storm. The menu includes sparkling, white, red, pink and skin contact wines, as well as sherries and fortified wines – but you don't need to be a connoisseur to appreciate what's on offer and staff will help guide you. There are also cocktails and beer if you fancy something that isn't wine. And if a 'quick drink' turns into quite a few more, there are small plates and those aforementioned cheese toasties (Cheddar and 'nduja, for example) to keep you going all evening. Want something more substantial? Its second branch, in Bethnal Green, is bigger and has a full restaurant menu and plenty of wine, too.

193 Hackney Road, E2 8JL
Other locations: Bethnal Green
sagerandwilde.com
@sagerandwilde

Happiness Forgets

Don't be alarmed if you get to the spot where Happiness Forgets is on a map and you can't find it. You'll need to head down the stairs from street level to access this basement boozer next to Hoxton Square. Once inside, you'll see dark red brick walls, moody lighting and a very, very well-stocked bar. Take a pew on a comfy sofa or booth, or grab a seat at the bar to watch the talented mixologists do their thing. This is a proper cocktail bar, so expect top-class drinks that offer a twist on classics, such as a Negroni made with olive vermouth, or a Tokyo Collins with yuzu sake and grapefruit juice. That said, if you're after a classic, or something that isn't on the menu, just ask the bar staff and they'll happily oblige. There's also wine, beer and non-alcoholic cocktails, so there's no danger of you going thirsty.

8–9 Hoxton Square, N1 6NU
happinessforgets.com
@happiness_hoxton

The Chesham Arms

The Chesham Arms

There's a lot to love about this east London watering hole on a quiet residential street in Hackney. A vibrant atmosphere, local beer on tap and the option to order in from London legends Yard Sale Pizza, for a start. With its eclectic decor (spot the Kellogg's radio and royal wedding mugs), fireplaces and a higgledy-piggledy stack of board games, the vibe here is cosy and welcoming. And that's before you get into the pub's heartwarming backstory. Back in 2012, a plan to turn it into flats sparked a two-year legal battle by the Save The Chesham group, as the community came together to protect it. Thanks to their hard work, the pub is still standing and was even awarded 'Asset of Community Value' status. Pop in for a drink and you'll soon see why the locals fought so hard to keep it going.

15 Mehetabel Road, E9 6DU
cheshamarms.com
@cheshamarms

The Pembury Tavern

Originally built in 1866, this pub was taken over by Five Points Brewing Company in 2018 and given a modern makeover. The local brewery takes its name from the five-points junction where this boozer sits – and while its new owners spruced up the decor, they kept its essence as a good old-fashioned pub. If you feel like getting competitive over pints, make a beeline for the old billiards table, or check out the wooden sideboard that's stuffed with board games. Naturally, the beer selection includes plenty of Five Points' own brews, but there's also a changing selection of guest beers, alongside wine, spirits, cocktails and soft drinks. Hungry? The pub's pizza really hits the spot, with loads of veggie and vegan options and a mix of interesting flavours (chilli honey, sesame crusts, housemade vegan 'nduja). Look out for tap takeover events and put your general knowledge to the test at the Monday pub quiz.

90 Amhurst Road, E8 1JH
pemburytavern.co.uk
@pemburytavern

The Castle Cinema

The antidote to the corporate multiplex, The Castle Cinema
is a community-focused, independent gem. This space first
opened as a cinema in 1913 – since then, it's been a bingo hall,
a warehouse and a snooker hall. In 2016, it went full circle
when a local couple started a crowdfunding campaign to restore
it to its former cinematic glory. And boy, is it glorious – gold
ornate detailing on the ceiling, two screening rooms with comfy
armchair seats and a gorgeous Art Deco bar. The programme
offers a mix of mainstream and indie films, as well as screenings
for parents and babies, those with dementia, autism and the
hearing-impaired. Got a real passion for cinema? Geek out in the
bar and delve into the archive of *Sight & Sound* magazines from
the 1960s to the present day.

First Floor, 64–66 Brooksby's Walk, E9 6DA
thecastlecinema.com
@thecastlecinema
☺ 🏛

God's Own Junkyard

Don't be put off by the name – you won't find a load of old junk
at this neon wonderland. Filled with luminous treasures, God's
Own Junkyard was set up by renowned neon artist Chris Bracey.
Having started out by making signs for Soho's bars and strip
clubs in the 70s and 80s, Bracey became known as 'Neon Man'.
He went on to make neon props for Hollywood films, working
with the likes of Stanley Kubrick, Tim Burton and Christopher
Nolan. He sadly passed away in 2014, but this Walthamstow
warehouse stuffed with his legendary creations celebrates his
legacy. There's also a bar and café, as well as Wild Card Brewery
and Mother's Ruin Gin Palace nearby. And despite all those neon
lights presumably running up an eye-watering electricity bill,
it's free to visit.

Unit 12, Ravenswood Industrial Estate, Shernhall Street, E17 9HQ
godsownjunkyard.co.uk
@godsownjunkyard
☺ ✪

Museum of London Docklands

Did you know that London was once the world's biggest port? That's what the Museum of London Docklands explores, charting the city's history through its docks. Housed in an old Georgian sugar warehouse, visitors can watch archive footage of a busy warehouse, get creeped out by a mummified cat and rat from the 1890s that were found around the docks, or see the kinds of swords used by the West India Docks police. It's full of interesting facts (who knew that when the old London Bridge got torn down, it was made into cutlery?) and little ones can get interactive in the Mudlarks gallery. It hosts temporary shows alongside its permanent collection, which includes 'London, Sugar and Slavery' – an important exhibition examining the city's involvement in the transatlantic slave trade.

No.1 Warehouse,
West India Quay,
Hertsmere Road, E14 4AL
museumoflondon.org.uk
@museumoflondon
☺ ☆

Museum of the Home

Wander around this Hackney museum and you might find yourself stuck in the past. While not quite time travel, the Museum of the Home offers the next best thing with its 'Rooms Through Time' exhibit. Based on real London homes, the rooms are decorated with furniture, textiles and trinkets from particular eras, starting from the 1600s to the present day. There's the 1695 parlour, typical of those in houses built in the decades after the Great Fire of London in 1666, the 1970s front room with its mustard yellow wallpaper and crochet doilies and a 1998 loft-style apartment, all open plan and industrial in style. The museum also considers the idea of 'home' through its Home Galleries, which dig into people's experiences from the past and present. It's a unique and intriguing place which brings history to life.

136 Kingsland Road, E2 8EA
museumofthehome.org.uk
@museumofthehome
☺ ✪

Whitechapel Gallery

Way before they were big names in the art world, David Hockney, Gilbert & George and Richard Long all had their first shows at the Whitechapel Gallery. Since it opened in 1901, the gallery has aimed to bring great art to east London – something it's been doing for more than 100 years now. In fact, it's known for various firsts – in 1939, it was the first British gallery to show Pablo Picasso's 'Guernica' and in 1958, Jackson Pollock had his first major show here. Visit this East End institution for temporary exhibitions of contemporary art and check out its website for details of its events programme filled with interesting talks, workshops, film screenings and activities for kids. You never know, you might see an up-and-coming artist's first big show here.

77–82 Whitechapel High Street, E1 7QX
whitechapelgallery.org
@whitechapelgallery

☺ ✪

Beyond Retro

Hawaiian shirts, vintage trench coats and 80s dresses are just a handful of the secondhand delights you might find at Beyond Retro's Dalston shop. This massive space in an Art Deco building stocks more than 12,000 items, so whether you're after streetwear or a one-of-a-kind party dress, you're unlikely to leave empty-handed. Sustainability is key to everything Beyond Retro does, which is why you can bring in your own pre-loved items to get a discount on whatever you want to buy in-store. It also has branches on Brick Lane (alongside quite a few other vintage shops) and Oxford Street and hosts special pop-ups, workshops and events. This shop is proof that second-hand definitely isn't second-best.

92–100 Stoke Newington Road, N16 7XB
Other locations: Brick Lane,
Oxford Street, White City,
Coal Drops Yard
beyondretro.com
@beyondretro

The Common Press

There's something for everyone at The Common Press, an inclusive bookshop and café that champions LGBTQ+ culture. Its selection spans fiction, non-fiction, poetry, drama, memoir, graphic novels and children's books, with titles by gay, trans and non-binary writers, covering everything from black history to feminism. It's great for seeking out books from small and indie publishers, which you might not find elsewhere. There's also a café selling coffee and pastries and places to sit if you want to dip into your purchases straight away. The shop is part of a multidisciplinary venue – there's an events space downstairs that hosts speed-dating, zine workshops and more, as well as the Common Counter bar next door if you fancy a cocktail.

118 Bethnal Green Road, E2 6DG
glasshouse.london
@glasshouselondon
@TheCommonPress

Labour and Wait

With its forest green tiled exterior and monochrome signage, Labour and Wait is the sort of shop that you can't walk past without wanting to go in. It's just as aesthetically pleasing inside, too. Specializing in timeless, functionally-designed products, it's full of things you never knew you wanted, like a German breakfast knife with a curved blade and beautiful wooden handle, or a proper feather duster made with real ostrich feathers (apparently they have a natural static which attracts the dust). Its Redchurch Street location is the original shop but there are others at Dover Street Market and in Marylebone, as well as its workroom in Bethnal Green where you can do click and collect – a bit like an Argos, but way more chic.

85 Redchurch Street, E2 7DJ
Other locations: Marylebone, Dover Street Market,
Bethnal Green
labourandwait.co.uk
@labourandwait

Old Spitalfields Market

You wouldn't know it now, but back in the 1600s, Spitalfields was considered a rural part of London. That all started to change in 1666 after the Great Fire of London meant that market traders set up stalls outside the city gates, which encouraged people to move there. Today, the covered market is still in the same location, which was previously a field (hence the name). These days, it offers a mix of food and drink stalls, restaurants, bars, independent makers and big name shops. Sample one of London's best patties from Bleecker Burger, get a coffee from Climpson & Sons, or satiate your sweet tooth with a Crosstown doughnut. Shopping-wise, you'll find everything from secondhand vinyl to candles. It also hosts regular events and special markets for antiques (every Thursday), vinyl (every other Friday) and more.

16 Horner Square, E1 6EW
oldspitalfieldsmarket.com
@oldspitalfieldsmarket

Libreria

Tired of technology and constant notifications? You'll love Libreria, a bookshop just off Brick Lane, which operates a 'no phones' policy. The idea is to encourage people to properly connect with the books and browse the shop without distractions. Libreria takes a different approach to curation too, with shelves arranged into broad themes such as 'dark times', 'bad feminist' and 'time and space', to help you come across books you might not have picked up otherwise. The walls are lined with handmade shelves crafted from unfinished recycled wood and if you find something you like the look of, there are various nooks and crannies with seats and lights for reading. Keep an eye out for special shelves curated by authors, showcasing their recommended titles. And without Google to rely on, direct your questions to the friendly staff.

65 Hanbury Street, E1 5JP
libreria.io
@librerialondon

Libreria

Index

Acknowledgements

Thanks to my brilliant editor Stacey Cleworth for answering my *many* questions and being a joy to work with (and for approaching me about this book in the first place – I'm very glad I found your email when I came back to a chaotic inbox after a holiday). Thanks also to Emily Lapworth for transforming my Google docs into a beautiful book, and to Luke Albert for bringing it all to life with your excellent photography. And to everyone else at Quadrille who has helped bring this book to fruition, I am very grateful.

Thank you to the *Time Out* lot (shout out to the now-sadly-defunct Corridor crew!) for being great friends and colleagues. I've learned a lot from you all over the years, including lots of useful (and some useless) London knowledge. Special thanks to Laura who was a big help when I was deciding which places to include, and provided lots of advice on writing a book.

Thanks to all my friends for being so supportive and never (seemingly) getting bored of me talking about this book. I'm especially grateful to Natalie for always cheering me on from afar (and listening to my very long voice notes), and to Sophie for all the book-writing support via WhatsApp.

To Clara, Dorothy, Jake, Lottie, Mum and Dad – thank you for your endless encouragement and advice. I'd like to say a special thank you to my Mum, who was the first person to teach me about the craft of writing and editing.

Finally, to my husband Charlie, thank you for your unwavering support, for always believing in me and for being my in-house sub-editor. The many cups of tea you made during the book-writing process were much appreciated, too.

Managing Director • Sarah Lavelle

Commissioning Editor • Stacey Cleworth

Art Direction & Design • Emily Lapworth

Designer • Sarah Fisher

Photographer • Luke Albert

Head of Production • Stephen Lang

Production Controller • Martina Georgieva

Published in 2023 by Quadrille
an imprint of Hardie Grant Publishing

Quadrille
52–54 Southwark Street
London SE1 1UN
quadrille.com

Cataloguing in Publication Data: a catalogue record for this book is available from the British Library.

Text © Isabelle Aron 2023
Photography © Luke Albert 2023
Design © Quadrille 2023

ISBN 9781787138957

Printed in China